LAST CHANCE TO SEE | ENDANGERED PLACES

ANITA GANERI

WAYLAND
www.waylandbooks.co.uk

LAST CHANCE TO SEE | ENDANGERED PLACES

Published in paperback in Great Britain
in 2019 by Wayland
Copyright © Wayland, 2017
All rights reserved

Editor: Sarah Silver
Designer: Alessandro Minoggi

ISBN: 978 1 5263 0300 4

FSC
www.fsc.org

MIX
Paper from
responsible sources
FSC® C104740

Printed and bound in Dubai

Wayland, an imprint of
Hachette Children's Group
Part of Hodder and Stoughton
Carmelite House
50 Victoria Embankment
London EC4Y 0DZ

An Hachette UK Company
www.hachette.co.uk
www.hachettechildrens.co.uk

Picture credits: Africa Images/istockphoto: 3tl, 21t.
Alexirina27000/Dreamstime: 10c. Andrey Armyagov/
Shutterstock: 22-23. BlackAperture/istockphoto: 9t. S.
Borison/Shutterstock: 28. Byelikova/Dreamstime: 3bl, 26-27.
Rich Carey/Shutterstock: 15t. Sam Dcruz/Shutterstock: 17t.
Ulrich Doering/Alamy: 17b. Mikhail Dudarev/Shutterstock:
20b. Emotionart/Dreamstime: 5b. EPA/Alamy: 12b.
fightbegin/istockphoto: 19t. Gustavo Frazao/Shutterstock: 6-7.
Frontpage/Shutterstock: 6b, 7t. Martin Froyda/Shutterstock:
10-11. Jonpaul Hosking/Shutterstock: 15b. Anton Ivanov/
Shutterstock: 3cl, 24-25. Debra James/Dreamstime: 3tr, 14-15.
Jim Keir/Alamy: 27t. Heiko Kiera/Shutterstock: 13t. Andrezej
Kubik/Shutterstock: 16-17. Andrey_Kuzmin/Shutterstock: front
cover br, 2. Kyodo/PAI: 25t. Frans Lanting/Getty Images: 20-
21. Chumash Maxim/Shutterstock: 22. Claudio Momberto/
Dreamstime: 16b. Mircea Nicolescu/Dreamstime: 3cr, 18-19.
Parafox/Shutterstock: front cover tr. photoloni/Shutterstock:
11t. Vincenzo Pinto/AFP/Getty Images: 29bl. PlusONE/
Shutterstock: 29tr. pzAxe/Shutterstock: 4b. Rex Features/
Shutterstock: 23t, 25b. Salko3p/Shutterstock: front cover
bl. Silken Photography/Shutterstock: 4-5. David Silverman/
Getty Images: 10b. VanderWold Images/Shutterstock: 5t.
Christopher Wood/Shutterstock: 8-9. Vladimir Wrangel/
Shutterstock: 21b. Alita Xander/Dreamstime: 12-13.

Every attempt has been made to clear copyright.
Should there be any inadvertent omission, please
apply to the Publisher for rectification.

The website addresses (URLs) included in this book
were valid at the time of going to press. However, it is
possible that contents or addresses may have changed
since the publication of this book. No responsibility
for any such changes can be accepted by either
the author or the Publisher.

CONTENTS

ON THE EDGE

Right across planet Earth, hundreds of amazing places are in danger of being lost. They include natural wonders, such as rainforest and mountains, together with historic buildings and cities. If they disappear, we will lose some of the world's most beautiful and varied wild places, along with people's homes and habitats for plants and animals.

WHAT'S HAPPENING?

Some places are at risk from natural dangers, such as erosion, but the threats mostly come from human activities, like pollution, overcrowding, illegal logging, hunting and fishing. One of the greatest threats facing the planet is global warming. Many scientists think that the Earth is getting warmer because of the greenhouse effect.

Pollution in the Yamuna River, India.

WARMING UP

The burning of fossil fuels, such as coal, oil and gas, is raising the amount of carbon dioxide in the atmosphere. Small amounts of carbon dioxide and other greenhouse gases, such as methane, are found naturally in the atmosphere. They play a vital role in keeping the Earth at the right temperature, by trapping the Sun's heat (similar to the panes of glass in a greenhouse) and stopping it escaping into space. But too much carbon dioxide is making the Earth too warm.

The city of Venice is a World Heritage site.

WORLD HERITAGE SITES

Many of the places in this book are World Heritage sites. This means that the United Nations (UN) has recognised them as having outstanding cultural, historical or scientific importance for the whole world. These places are given special protection, but if they are under threat, they can be placed on an 'in danger' list to receive extra help.

AMAZON RAINFOREST

The world's largest rainforest grows along the banks of the Amazon River in South America. The forest is an extraordinarily rich habitat, with one in ten of all known species of plants and animals on Earth living there. It is also home to hundreds of groups of indigenous people.

STATS

LOCATION: South America

AREA: 6 million sq km

FOREST TYPE: Tropical rainforest

MAIN RIVER: Amazon (6,400 km)

THREATENED BY:
Cattle ranching, logging, gold mining, road building

VANISHING FOREST

Since 1978, over 750,000 sq km of the Amazon rainforest have been cut down. The Amazon rainforest still makes up more than half of all the rainforest left on Earth. However, if the current rate of destruction continues, rainforests could disappear completely in 40 years' time.

FOREST TO FARM

Brazil is one of the world's largest producers of beef, and cattle ranching is the main reason why the Amazon rainforest is under threat. Vast areas (around 60 per cent) of the forest have been cut down, burned and turned into pasture. Today, there are some 90 million cattle in the Amazon.

CARBON CONTROLLER

During photosynthesis, rainforest trees soak up huge amounts of carbon dioxide, helping to keep it in check. If the trees are chopped down, this control is lost and the amount of carbon dioxide in the atmosphere increases, leading to further global warming.

URGENT ACTION

Using satellite technology, experts are monitoring the Amazon rainforest. They are working with conservationists and governments to find ways of stopping the destruction. One idea is to promote sustainable farming that does not damage the forest, but allows local people to make a living.

ARCTIC

The Arctic lies in the northernmost part of the world, inside the Arctic Circle. It has one of the harshest climates on Earth, with temperatures falling to -70°C. The Arctic is so cold that, for most of the year, the Arctic Ocean is covered in a thick layer of ice.

SHRINKING ICE

The amount of ice covering the Arctic Ocean naturally varies with the seasons, expanding in winter and shrinking in spring and summer. Since 1979, however, satellites have shown that the ice is melting faster than ever. In fact, some scientists predict that, within a few years, the Arctic Ocean will be ice-free by the end of each summer.

STATS

LOCATION: Canada, Russia, USA, Greenland, Norway, Sweden, Finland

AREA: Around 14 million sq km

AVERAGE TEMPERATURES: 0°C (summer), -40°C (winter)

SEA ICE THICKNESS: 2-3 metres

THREATENED BY: Global warming, pollution, mining, illegal fishing

The number of polar bears is diminishing because there isn't enough ice for them to hunt on.

WARMING WORLD

Many scientists think that global warming is causing the Earth's temperature to rise. This is heating the air over the Arctic and causing the sea ice and the Greenland ice sheet (left) to melt. If the melting continues, sea levels around the world will rise, flooding low-lying places.

CLIMATE CONTROL

The ice at the Arctic plays an important part in controlling the world's weather and climate. Because sea ice is white, it reflects sunlight back into space, keeping the region cool. The cool air is also carried around the world, helping to regulate the temperature globally.

URGENT ACTION

Governments around the world are working to tackle the problem of global warming. Meanwhile, scientists are using satellites to collect data about the extent and temperature of the ice, and how it is moving. This is fed into computers to predict what will happen in the future.

DEAD SEA

Located between Jordan, Israel and Palestine, the Dead Sea is actually a salt lake. It is the lowest point on Earth, lying some 420 metres below sea level. The lake is almost ten times saltier than the sea, making it a harsh place for plants and animals to live in, but a beautiful and unusual place for people to visit.

The Dead Sea is so salty that you float on its surface.

DRAINING AWAY

The Dead Sea is shrinking dangerously fast, with the surface level dropping by more than a metre each year. Environmentalists are warning that, at the current rate, the lake could disappear altogether by 2050. To reach the shoreline today, visitors have to travel about two kilometres from the rocks that originally marked the water level.

The Ein Gedi resort once stood on the lake shore. Today, a special shuttle takes tourists down to the water's edge.

WATER SUPPLY

Apart from a few flash floods in the short rainy season, the lake's only water supply is the River Jordan. Over the past 50 years, however, so much water has been taken from the river for drinking and irrigating farmers' fields that the amount flowing into the Dead Sea has been greatly reduced.

STATS

LOCATION: Jordan, Israel, Palestine

AREA: 605 SQ KM

DEPTH: 304 M

HEIGHT BELOW SEA LEVEL: 420M

THREATENED BY: Loss of water, dam building on the River Jordan

SINKING FEELING

As the Dead Sea shrinks, hundreds of sinkholes (above) are appearing on the shore. Some of the sinkholes are as big as baseball fields, or as deep as two-storey houses. They form when a thick, ancient layer of salt underneath the newly dry land collapses. Sinkholes have already swallowed up factories and tourist resorts, and the problem is getting worse.

URGENT ACTION

One plan for saving the Dead Sea is to build an enormous pipeline that would bring sea water across the desert, from the Red Sea. The water would first have to be desalinated, because otherwise it would damage the Dead Sea's unique chemical make-up. The so-called 'Red-Dead Project' would be a huge feat of engineering and extremely costly for the countries involved.

EVERGLADES

A huge area of tropical wetlands in in Florida, USA, the Everglades is made up of mangroves, marshes, pine woods, rivers and lakes. About a fifth of the Everglades is protected as a national park and is home to endangered species, such as manatees, alligators and panthers.

DRAINING AWAY

Today, the Everglades is only about half the size it was a century ago. As more and more people have moved into the area, the Everglades has come under great pressure. Its water has been drained off for factories, sugarcane farms and to supply thousands of new homes.

STATS

LOCATION: FLORIDA, USA

AREA (OF NATIONAL PARK): 6,105 SQ KM

TYPE OF HABITAT: WETLANDS

LARGEST LAKE: OKEECHOBEE (1,900 SQ KM)

THREATENED BY: DRAINAGE, POLLUTION, INTRODUCED SPECIES

DIRTY WATER

Lake Okeechobee, the huge, freshwater lake at the heart of the Everglades, is at serious risk from pollution. Chemicals from fertilisers used on the surrounding farmland are washed into the water. Small plants, called algae, feed on the chemicals and bloom, forming huge scummy mats on the surface of the water, and poisoning fish and other wildlife.

An algal bloom on Lake Okeechobee.

UNWELCOME VISITORS

Another big problem facing the Everglades is the introduction of plants and animals that do not normally live there. These upset the delicate balance of the wildlife in the park. Plants, such as Brazilian pepper, grow very quickly and crowd out local plants. Thousands of exotic pets, such as Burmese pythons (left), have also escaped or been released into the park. They prey on local mammals, including raccoons and bobcats.

URGENT ACTION

In 2000, the US government launched an ambitious plan to clean up the Everglades' water supply and protect its wildlife within 30 years. Billions of dollars were set aside. The main aim is to let more freshwater flow through the region, but progress has been very slow and the Everglades remains on the list of UN World Heritage sites in danger.

GREAT BARRIER REEF

The biggest coral reef system in the world, the Great Barrier Reef runs for more than 2,300 km along the north-east coast of Australia. It is home to a huge variety of life, including over 2,000 different species of fish. The reef was built over thousands of years by tiny coral polyps no bigger than fingernails.

CORAL IN CRISIS

The Great Barrier Reef has lost more than half of its coral since 1985, with two thirds of the loss happening in the last 20 years. There are many dangers facing the reef. Oil spills from ships, pollution from farm run-off, and the damage done by tropical cyclones are all serious problems, but the greatest threat is global warming.

STATS

LOCATION: AUSTRALIA

LENGTH: 2,300 KM

AREA: 350,000 SQ KM

NUMBER OF REEFS: MORE THAN 2,900

THREATENED BY: CORAL BLEACHING, GLOBAL WARMING, STARFISH

CORAL BLEACHING

It is thought that almost one quarter of the Great Barrier Reef has been killed by coral bleaching (left). This happens when the sea temperature rises because of global warming. Corals live in partnership with algae that give them their colour. If the water gets too warm, the coral spit the algae out and turn white. The algae also supply the coral with food. Without them, the coral may starve and die.

STARFISH STRIKE

Another threat to the reef comes from prickly crown-of-thorns starfish, which feed on coral. Recently, the number of starfish has grown dramatically and huge patches of the reef have been destroyed. This may be because the starfishes' natural predators, such as giant triton sea snails, have been overfished, or because the starfish are thriving in the polluted water.

A crown-of-thorns starfish.

URGENT ACTION

One of the latest ideas to protect the Great Barrier Reef is a robot that has been trained to find and kill crown-of-thorns starfish. Once it spots a starfish, it will extend its needle-capped arm and give the starfish a lethal injection of poison. One robot can carry enough poison to kill 200 starfish.

KILIMANJARO

Kilimanjaro is the highest mountain in Africa, the largest in a line of volcanoes at the end of the Rift Valley. Even though Kilimanjaro is so close to the equator, its peak is covered in glaciers. But they are melting at a startling pace, and could possibly disappear for good.

MELTING MOUNTAIN

Kilimanjaro is sometimes called the 'shining mountain' because of the ice on its summit. But its nickname may soon have to change. More than 80 per cent of the ice cap has been lost since it was first measured in 1912. Climbers have reported seeing chunks of ice as big as rooms breaking off the glaciers.

Once covered in glaciers, Kilimanjaro's cone-shaped peak now has little of its ice cap remaining.

PEAK DESTRUCTION

Global warming is taking its toll on the glaciers but other factors are also to blame. One of the biggest problems is the loss of forests on the mountain's lower slopes. These are being destroyed by man-made fires, which is having a serious effect on the local weather. Fewer trees means less moisture is pumped into the atmosphere, leading to fewer clouds and less rain to freeze into ice on the mountain top.

STATS

LOCATION: Tanzania
HEIGHT: 5,895 metres
MOUNTAIN TYPE: Volcano
LAST ERUPTION: None recorded
THREATENED BY:
Global warming, forest clearance

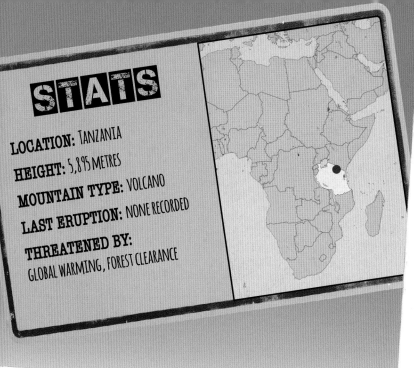

DARK ICE

With no new ice being made, the old glacier is turning dirty and grey. Darker surfaces soak up more sunlight than lighter surfaces, which also speeds up the melting. Scientists are monitoring the ice closely, using aerial photographs and taking ice samples. Some of the ice is estimated to be more than 10,000 years old.

Fires are used to clear the forest for farmland.

URGENT ACTION

One plan scientists have come up with to save the remaining glaciers is to cover the ice with a bright, white plastic cover. This would seal the glaciers and reflect sunlight back into space. The idea has already been tried on glaciers in Switzerland.

MACHU PICCHU

Perched on a high ridge in the Andes Mountains, Machu Picchu was built by the Incas around 550 years ago, but lay abandoned for centuries. It was rediscovered in 1911, and has since become a major tourist attraction. Tens of thousands of people visit every year.

MASTER BUILDERS

Experts think that Machu Picchu may have been built as a religious site or fortress. The ruins of palaces, squares, temples and homes clearly show the great skill of the Inca builders. Using only simple tools, they carved stones into blocks, which fitted together perfectly, even without cement.

STATS

LOCATION: Peru

ALTITUDE: 2,430 m

FOUNDED: Around 1450

STATUS: World Heritage Site (since 1983)

THREATENED BY: Tourism, pollution

TOURIST TRAIL

For centuries, Machu Picchu lay hidden from sight, but it is now the most visited tourist attraction in Peru. The number of tourists has increased dramatically, from around 6,000 annually in 1984 to over one million today. The sheer numbers of people are putting Machu Picchu under pressure from overcrowding, litter and pollution.

Most people travel by bus along this road to reach Machu Picchu.

UNDER PRESSURE

In the 1990s, the government of Peru approved plans to build a cable car to Machu Picchu to bring in more tourists. Many people protested against the plan, because of the damage it would do to the site, so it was put on hold. Flights over the ruins have also been banned.

URGENT ACTION

Today, tourism is being more carefully monitored to try to preserve Machu Picchu. Only 2,500 tourists are allowed into the city every day. Visitors may also be asked to wear soft shoes to reduce the pressure on the crumbling ruins.

MADAGASCAR

Madagascar is the fourth largest island in the world. The island faces many threats, especially the loss of its forests which is causing catastrophic soil erosion. This is putting not only people's livelihoods at risk, but also Madagascar's unique wildlife – many of its plants and animals are found nowhere else on Earth.

VANISHING FORESTS

Since humans arrived in Madagascar around 2,350 years ago, more than 90 per cent of its forests have been lost. Most have been cut down to make way for slash-and-burn farming by local people. Trees are also turned into charcoal, which is used as fuel for cooking, and large areas have been cleared for coffee plantations.

STATS

LOCATION: Indian Ocean

CAPITAL: Antananarivo

SIZE: 587,041 SQ KM

UNIQUE ANIMAL SPECIES: Over 1,000

THREATENED BY: Deforestation, Soil Erosion

WASHED AWAY

The forest trees anchor the soil with their roots. When they are cut down, the soil is easily washed away by heavy rains. On Madagascar, millions of tonnes of soil are being lost every year. Many people on the island rely on farming for food and to make a living, so the loss of soil is disastrous.

The extensive erosion on the island has led to it being called the Great Red Island.

LOST HABITAT

Deforestation and soil loss are having a devastating effect on Madagascar's unique wildlife, including its famous lemurs (below). Habitat loss, together with hunting and illegal logging, are hitting them very hard. Today, around 90 per cent of lemurs are threatened with extinction, with more than 23 species labelled critically endangered.

URGENT ACTION

One plan to save this extraordinary island and its wildlife is to plant new areas of forest with trees specially grown in nurseries. Already, millions of trees have been planted, creating new habitats for lemurs and other animals. The aim is to plant billions more in the next ten years.

MALDIVES

The Maldives are a group of low-lying, small coral islands only 298 sq km in size, but spread over around 90,000 sq km of sea. With their idyllic location and sandy beaches, the Maldives are a popular holiday spot. But rapidly rising sea levels are putting these beautiful islands and the lives of the islanders at risk.

LYING LOW

Most of the islands lie less than 2 m above sea level, making the Maldives the world's lowest-lying country. As sea levels rise, the islands are in serious danger. Environmental experts predict that global warming could cause sea levels to rise by nearly 60 cm by 2100, leaving most of the islands underwater.

WALLED CITY

The islanders face an uncertain future. Already, a 30-metre-long wall has been built around the capital, Malé, to keep the water out. The government of the Maldives is also working hard to cut the country's greenhouse gas emissions, but such a small nation cannot solve the problem of global warming alone – it needs the world's support.

CRUMBLING COASTS

Flooding is not the only danger facing the Maldives. The seas are getting warmer, killing off the islands' coral reefs. The reefs are home to thousands of species of animals, but they also act as a barrier to protect the coasts from being worn away by tropical storms and tsunamis.

In 2004, the islands were devastated by the tsunami that swept across the Indian Ocean.

STATS

LOCATION: Indian Ocean

AREA: 298 SQ KM

POPULATION: 393,000

CAPITAL CITY: Malé

THREATENED BY: Rising sea levels, global warming, coastal erosion

URGENT ACTION

One plan the government of the Maldives is looking at, is to buy up land in another country, such as India or Australia, and move the whole population there. Another is to build a number of artificial, floating islands that will stay above water as sea levels rise.

PALMYRA

The city of Palmyra in Syria was one of the most important cultural centres of the ancient world. Located in a desert oasis, it stood at the crossroads of several trade routes. Today, however, it stands in the middle of a war zone, and many of its historic buildings have been destroyed.

ANCIENT HISTORY

Palmyra came under Roman rule in the 1st century CE. It quickly grew in importance because of its location on the trade route between Persia, China, India and the Roman Empire. The centre of the city was a grand, straight street, lined with tall columns. Along it stood the city's major buildings, including temples, the market place and theatre.

STATS

LOCATION: SYRIA

FOUNDED: 2000 BCE

ABANDONED: 1932

MOST FAMOUS BUILDING:
TEMPLE OF BEL

THREATENED BY:
CIVIL WAR, MINOR EARTHQUAKES

The Temple of Baalshamin was destroyed in August 2015.

WAR-TORN CITY

Palmyra was already at risk from earthquakes and the growth of a nearby town. But, in 2011, civil war broke out in Syria. Palmyra was captured and many buildings destroyed. Some of the artefacts from the city's museum had already been taken away for safe-keeping, but others were smashed to pieces or stolen.

ARCH OF TRIUMPH

One of the buildings destroyed in the war was the Arch of Triumph, dating from Roman times. In 2016, a model of the Arch was made from marble, cut to exactly the same shape and design as the original, based on 3D photographs. It is being taken on tour to world cities, and then hopefully to Palmyra, where it will stand near the site of the original arch.

A reconstruction of the Arch of Triumph on display in London.

URGENT ACTION

Experts are monitoring the situation in Palmyra closely to see how much of the site is left. But, until the war ends and the area is cleared of mines and bombs, there is very little that they can do. There are hopes that destroyed buildings can eventually be restored, using 3D photography and the original stones.

TAJ MAHAL

The Taj Mahal was commissioned by the Mughal Emperor Shah Jahan as a tomb for his wife, Mumtaz Mahal, who died in 1631. Built from white marble and inlaid with semi-precious stones, it stands on the bank of the Yamuna River.
It attracts around eight million visitors a year.

TURNING YELLOW

Once gleaming white, the marble of the Taj Mahal is being stained yellow by serious air pollution in Agra. The pollution is largely caused by fumes from vehicles and factories, but also from the burning of the city's rubbish and from a nearby crematorium. Another source is burning fumes from the cow dung, that people use as fuel for cooking and heating.

POLLUTED RIVER

Another danger facing the Taj Mahal is insect droppings, which are turning the marble green. Swarms of insects breed in the nearby Yamuna River (below). They are usually kept in check by fish, but today, the river is so polluted that the fish are dying. Workers scrub the walls clean every day but this is taking the sheen off the marble.

STATS

LOCATION: Agra, India

BUILT: 1632–1648

HEIGHT: 73 m

NUMBER OF VISITORS: 7–8 million per year

THREATENED BY: Pollution, insect droppings, tourism

CRACKING UP

Growing demand for water is draining the river dry and putting the Taj Mahal at risk. The Taj's foundations are made from wood and need to be kept moist to stop them from becoming brittle and breaking apart. Already, cracks have appeared in parts of the tomb, and the minarets have shown signs of tilting.

URGENT ACTION

Archaeologists have come up with an ingenious way of turning the marble white again. Every few years, they plaster on layers of fuller's earth (a type of clay), mixed with water. This is based on a traditional Indian beauty treatment. The clay is left on the walls to dry, then removed, and the surfaced is washed with purified water.

VENICE

The beautiful city of Venice sits on a group of small islands in a lagoon, linked by canals and bridges. Today, Venice is one of the most visited cities in the world, with millions of tourists visiting every year. But the city is slowly sinking and its future is at serious risk.

STORY OF VENICE

During the Middle Ages, Venice was a major sea power because of its location on the Adriatic Sea. It was also a flourishing centre of art and trade. This made Venice very wealthy and, by the late 13th century, it was the richest city in Europe. Its leading families competed with each other to build the grandest palaces.

LOCATION: ITALY

AREA: 414.5 SQ KM

POPULATION: 265,000

MAIN CANAL: GRAND CANAL

THREATENED BY:
FLOODING, TOURISM

SINKING FEELING

Venice floods regularly because of high tides, but the risk of flooding is increasing, as global warming causes sea levels to rise. In addition, the city is sinking at a rate of around 1-2 mm a year, because so much water has been taken from underground. This threatens the foundations of centuries-old buildings and could swamp parts of the city altogether.

Raised paths have been installed, so people can walk over the flood water.

TOO MANY TOURISTS

Tens of thousands of tourists visit Venice every day, and many arrive on huge cruise ships. The ships sail close to the city centre, causing serious damage to the city's wooden foundations, as well as creating large amounts of pollution. There are calls to have the largest ships banned from the lagoon or for a new port to be built further away from the city.

Once in place, the barrier should protect Venice for one century.

URGENT ACTION

To stop the city from flooding, a gigantic barrier is being built. It is made up of 78 huge gates that will be fixed across the three entrances to the lagoon. The gates will be able to be opened and closed to regulate the amount of water flowing in from the sea.

GLOSSARY

3D PHOTOGRAPHY
Using photography to capture a 3-dimensional picture of something.

AERIAL
Something that happens in the air or from the air.

ARTEFACTS
Objects made by people that give us information about the past.

BLEACH
Turn something white or lighter by chemicals or sunlight.

CHARCOAL
A black coal-like substance made by heating wood; it is used as fuel.

CONSERVATIONIST
A person who works to protect the natural world and its wildlife.

CREMATORIUM
A place where a dead person's body is cremated, or burnt.

DEFORESTATION
Deliberate cutting down of forests to use land for grazing or agriculture.

DESALINATE
To remove salt from seawater.

ECOSYSTEM
A place and the plants and animals that live in it, and depend on each other.

EQUATOR
An imaginary line running around the middle of the Earth.

EROSION
When something is worn away by the wind, water or waves.

FOSSIL FUELS
Natural fuels such as coal, oil or gas, formed millions of years ago from the remains of living things.

GLOBAL WARMING
Average increase in temperature at the Earth's surface.

HABITAT
The natural home of a plant or animal.

IRRIGATE
Supply water to land so that crops can grow.

LAGOON
A stretch of seawater separated from the sea by a sandbank or coral reef.

MANGROVE
Tree that grows in coastal water and has roots above ground.

MINARET
A slender tower that is usually part of a mosque.

OASIS
A place in the desert where water is found and crops can grow.

PASTURE
Land covered in grass that is used for feeding animals on.

PHOTOSYNTHESIS
The process by which green plants make their own food, using sunlight, carbon dioxide and water.

PLANTATION
A huge farm on which crops, such as coffee, sugar and bananas, are grown.

POLLUTION
The process by which chemicals, litter or gases damage the environment.

POLYP
Tiny sea creature with acolumn-shaped body, and a mouth surrounded by a ring of tentacles.

PREDATOR
Animal that hunts other animals for food.

RUN-OFF
When water or chemicals drain away from the surface of the land.

SINKHOLES
Holes in the ground that are caused by water erosion and can suddenly appear.

SLASH-AND-BURN
A type of farming in which a patch of land is cleared by cutting down and burning vegetation before sewing seeds.

SUSTAINABLE
A way of life that exploits natural resources without destroying the ecological balance of an area.

WETLANDS
Land made up of swamps and marshes.

LOCATION MAP

ARCTIC

VENICE

PALMYRA

EVERGLADES

TAJ MAHAL

DEAD SEA

AMAZON RAINFOREST

KILIMANJARO

GREAT BARRIER REEF

MACHU PICCHU

MALDIVES

MADAGASCAR

FURTHER INFORMATION

WHC.UNESCO.ORG
The website of UNESCO (United Nations Educational, Scientific and Cultural Organization), with a list of its World Heritage sites.

WWW.WORLDWILDLIFE.ORG/PLACES
A section of the WWF (World Wildlife Fund) website, dedicated to endangered places around the world.

WWW.NATIONALGEOGRAPHIC.COM/TRAVEL/WORLD-HERITAGE/
A section of the National Geographic website, looking at World Heritage sites around the world.

INDEX